*Permanent Marker and Alcohol Ink Colors Run and Bleed like Magic with Alcohol!*

Coffee Filter Cards - page 11

Coffee Filter Votive Candle page 11

**Color with Markers - Technique #1 -** 1. Place a filter on a craft sheet or freezer paper (shiny side up) to protect your surface. Use Gold 'Scribbles' (or pour metallic Gold paint into a bottle with a needle point top). Draw the design. Let dry. • 2. Color as desired, leaving some open spaces. • 3. Lightly mist with Blending Solution. If desired smear colors with a brush or swab. Let dry. TIP: Enhance with more Gold paint or add more color as desired. Let dry.

**Technique #2 -** 1. Place a filter on a craft sheet or freezer paper (shiny side up). Draw with markers leaving some open space. Let dry. • 2. Lightly mist with alcohol to make the colors bleed. Let dry. • 3. Use Gold paint to outline shapes within the design. Let dry. Tip: Add more color as desired. Let dry.

## Beauty in the Ordinary

*by Barbara Buechley*

*This whole coffee filter idea evolved while I was teaching art for talented home schoolers. The experimental projects required inexpensive materials so when I cleaned out the coffee maker and noticed how durable, transparent, and flat coffee filters were, experimenting began.*

*By using colors of Permanent Markers - from both Copic and Sharpie plus Blending Solution or Alcohol - great color effects were created. I love the effect and so began another discovery of beauty in an everyday object.*

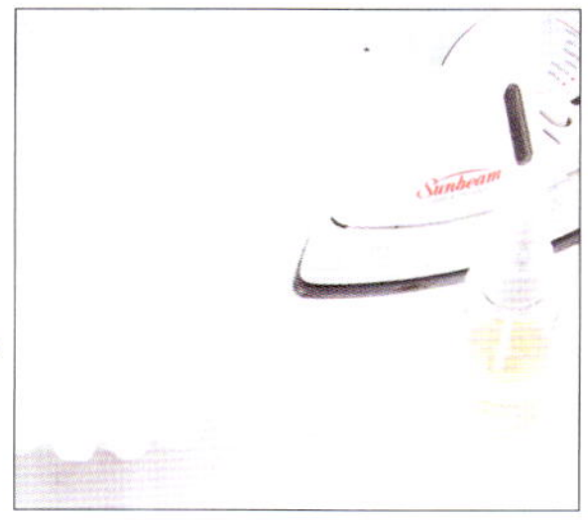

**Coffee Filters -**

Lightly spray a filter with water and press flat. Use White round coffee filters with fluted or pleated edges that are approximately 8" when flat. Permanent Markers and Alcohol Inks make great runs and bleeds on these.

# Coordinate Your Embellishments

*by Jen del Muro*

*Creating one of a kind projects just got more fun and now you can save money too! Turn plain and ordinary into dazzling! Waste no more time searching for the right color button, ribbon, or trim.*

*Now you can purchase plain white embellishments (which cost less) and color them with Permanent Markers from Copic to match your project. You can even color ribbon and it won't bleed onto your card or project. These markers also work wonderfully on buttons, metal and acrylic accents.*

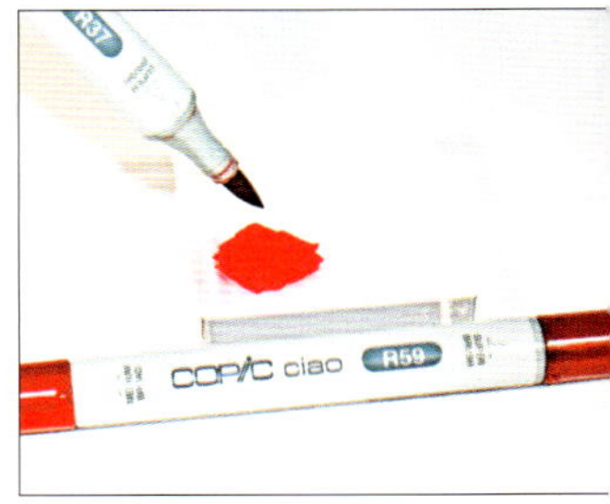

Goody Bag page 11

Ice Cream Cone - page 11

I Ruff You - page 11

Trick or Sweet page 11

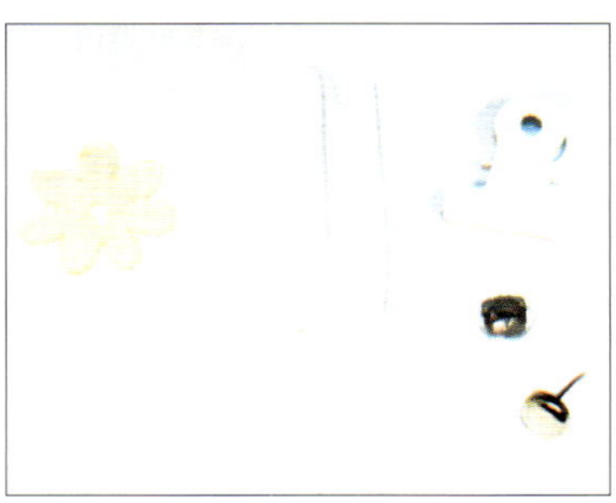

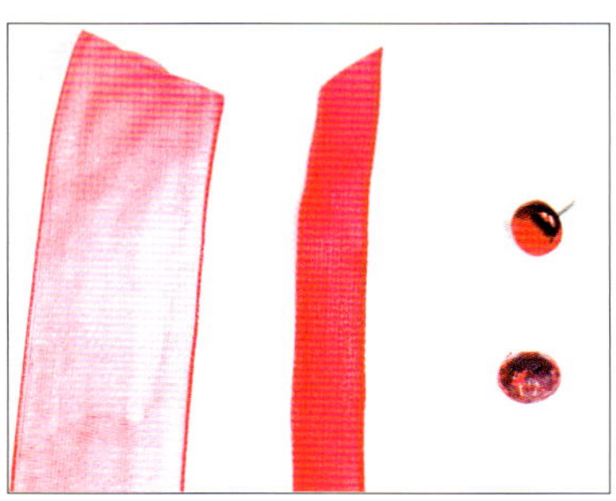

**Coordinate Your Embellishments**

1. Start with plain ribbons, brads, clips, buttons, and acrylic pieces. • 2. Both sheer ribbons and solid ribbons can be colored. You can even color brads and tacks. • 3. Everyday items such as buttons, plastic, and metal can be colored with Markers from *Copic*. Let the pieces dry before using them.

Happy 29th page 12

**Technique #1**
**Marker to Marker -**

Using the brush end of your lighter color, pick up ink from the chisel end of the darker color. Simply brush out all ink from the lighter marker after you are finished blending.

**Technique #2**
**Using a Palette -**

Clean acrylic blocks make great color palettes. Scribble some of the darker ink onto the palette and pick it up with the brush end of the lighter colored marker.

Thank You Fairy Much
page 11

Hey Sweetie - page 11

Have a Fairy Christmas
page 12

# Blending with Markers

*by Jen del Muro*

*Give your coloring a professional depth and beautiful dimension by blending colors to create areas of darker shadows and lighter highlights.*

*This easy technique makes a big difference in the final appearance of your cards, giving you that desired "wow" factor.*

**Blending Options**

There are 3 basic blending techniques. Try one of the 3 blending techniques for Markers from *Copic* that are shown on these pages.

**Technique #3**
**Blending Directly On Paper -**

Color an image with a lighter color.

Accent the images around the edges or in a shadow area with a darker color. Blend colors together by using small circles and feathering the darker color into the lighter color.

Clear Acrylic Album - page 12

**Clear Acrylic Album**

*Part of the fun in making a clear album lies in seeing through the clear pages. This is done by aligning photos and embellishments back-to back and creatively positioning papers, ribbons, and trims.*

1. Gather your materials - five 4" x 10" clear acrylic album pages from *AccuCut* • colors of Alcohol Ink, Blending Solution and Glossy Accents adhesive from *Ranger* • ATC clear Screen Prints from *Hambly Studios* • embellishments, 2-sided papers, Rub-on messages, 'Slick' marker, ribbons and trims from *American Crafts* • binding machine from *Zutter*. • 2. Use a cotton ball or applicator to dab colors of Alcohol Ink onto the back of clear Screen Prints. Let dry. • 3. Cut papers and photos to the desired size. Adhere to each page with Glossy Accents. • 4. Punch holes along one side of each page with a binding machine. • 5. Weave, lace or tie ribbon through the holes. Add embellishments to the pages with Glossy Accents. • 6. Secure pages together with a binder ring. Tie ribbon to the binder ring. Add additional embellishments as desired. Personalize your album with Rub-on messages and write on the clear acrylic pages with a Black 'Slick' marker.

1. Gather materials.

2. Color with Alcohol Ink.

3. Add papers and photos.

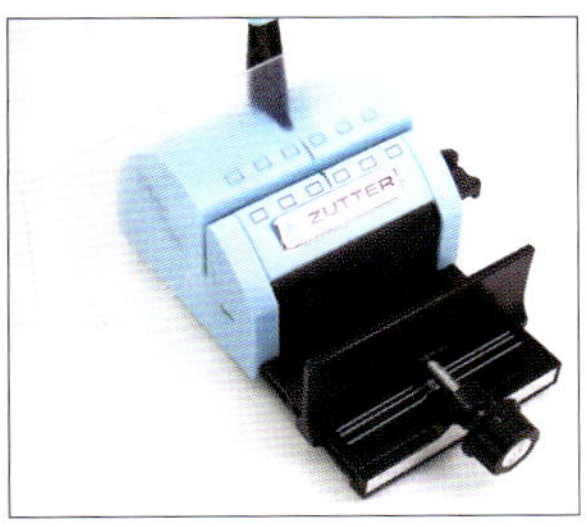

4. Punch holes in acrylic.

5. Lace and tie ribbons.

6. Embellish album.

Perpetual Calendar - page 13

Clear Acrylic Card - page 13

# Techniques on Clear Acrylic

*by Paula Phillips*

*You'll love working with clear acrylic surfaces... they are fun and creative to decorate.*

## Clear Acrylic Perpetual Calendar

*Here's a clear solution to your need to keep up with calendar dates. Because it's erasable, you'll never have to buy another calendar again.*

You will need a clear acrylic 'Perpetual Calendar' from *Petersen Arne*. • 1. On the back of the calendar, use painter's tape or masking tape to mask off the center of the month block and around the calendar center. • 2. Dab on the first color of Alcohol Ink from *Ranger* with a cotton ball or applicator. Let dry. Dab on the second color of Alcohol Ink. Let dry. Repeat with additional colors if desired. Let dry. Apply Glossy Accents over the Alcohol Inks with a brush to seal it. Let dry. • 3. Remove tape carefully so not to pull off the lines. Embellish with crystals, flowers, brads, clips and ribbons. • 4. Use an Expo or Sharpie marker from *Sanford* to write months, dates and events on the calendar. Remove writing with a cotton ball and Blending Solution.

Never Grow Up - page 13

Dance - Sing - Live - page 13

# Colors On Clear Acrylic

*by Jen del Muro*

*Colored acrylic possesses a transparency that is unequaled in any other medium, bringing to your project an airy, open feeling. Fans of acrylic appreciate its clarity, versatility, sturdiness, and beauty. If you have never worked with acrylic, this is your chance to experiment. Acrylic pieces are a fun and easy way to dress up any project. With Permanent Markers, you can simply color them to match.*

*Spritz a little Blending Solution on the colored acrylic pieces and watch them come to life!*

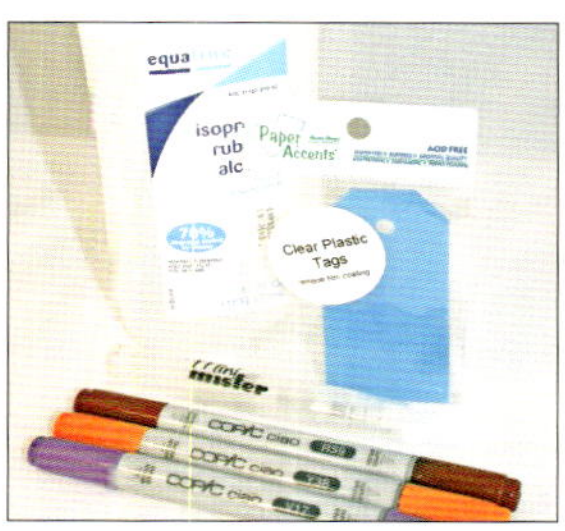

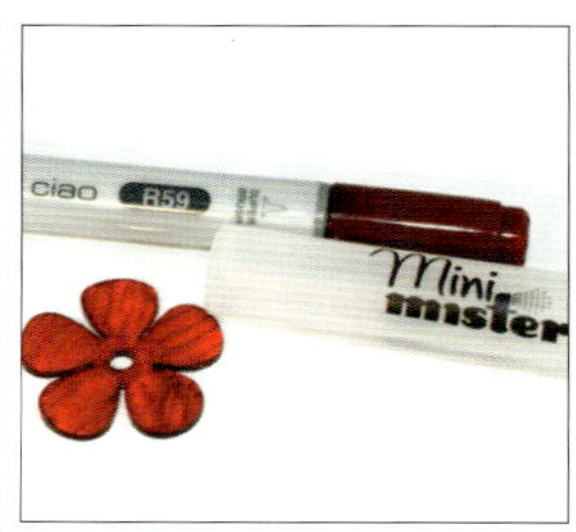

## Coloring on Clear Acrylic Tags

*Acrylic tags are an inexpensive and easy surface. Just peel off the protective surface and have fun.*
You will need acrylic tags, alcohol based markers, and a sprayer or Mini-mister filled with alcohol. • 1. Gather your materials and protect your work surface with a Craft Sheet or Freezer Paper (shiny side up). • 2. Peel off the protective surface. Color the back of a clear tag with color Markers from *Copic*. • 3. Spritz the colors with Blending Solution to create a texture and to make the colors blend. • 4. Stamp words on the front with Black StazOn ink. Let dry. Add ribbons. • 5. Color a clear acrylic flower with a Marker from *Copic*. Use a Mini Mister to spray it with Blending Solution. Let dry.

Tip The sheer ribbon on this project was originally a Cream color. Color ribbon with the same Purple marker or ink to match your project.

# Clear 'Stamp Blocks'

*by Jen del Muro*

*Turn an ordinary clear stamp block into something special. Simply color the underside of the block with Permanent Markers and Blending Solution for a great look.*

*Next time you need a small gift for someone special, consider these acrylic pieces. They are a perfect size for decorating a desk, cubicle, or refrigerator.*

## Acrylic Refrigerator Magnet

Let this quick gift inspire you to make several magnets in a variety of themes for your friends and family. 1. Color the underside of a clear acrylic stamp block with colored Markers from *Copic*. • 2. Spritz with Blending Solution to make the colors bleed and add texture. Let dry. • 3. Rubber stamp words on a piece of cardstock. Bend the edges of the paper up to wrap around the clear block. Adhere the cardstock to bottom and around the sides using double sided tape along the edges. Add ribbon trim around the edges. Trim as desired. 4. Hot glue a strong magnet to the back.

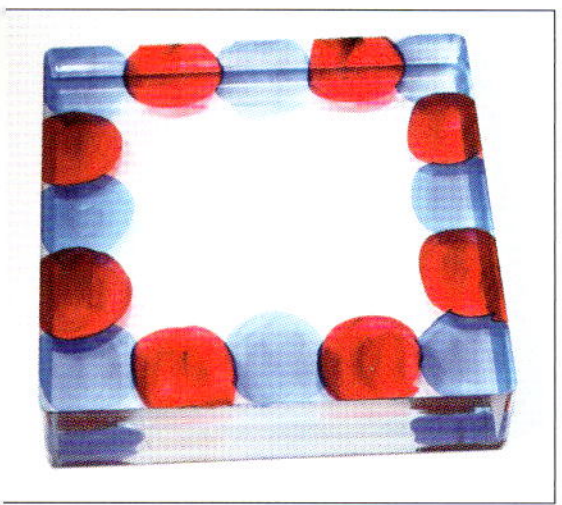

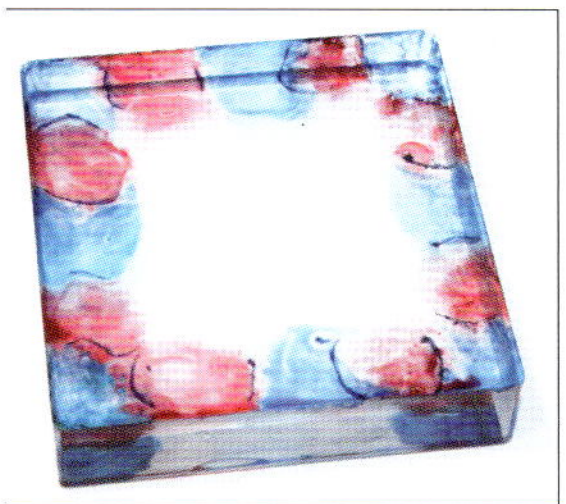

## Acrylic Paperweight

With the addition of a bit of color, you can turn an ordinary clear stamp block into a reminder of someone special.
1. On the underside of a clear stamp block, color dots with Markers from *Copic*. • 2. Spritz with Blending Solution to make the colors bleed. Let dry. • 3. Glue a photo behind the colors and up around the edges. Trim the edges with ribbon and rhinestones.

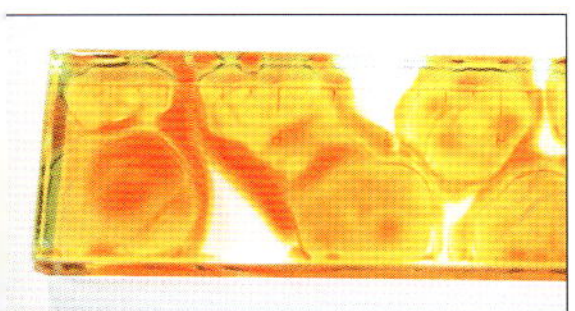

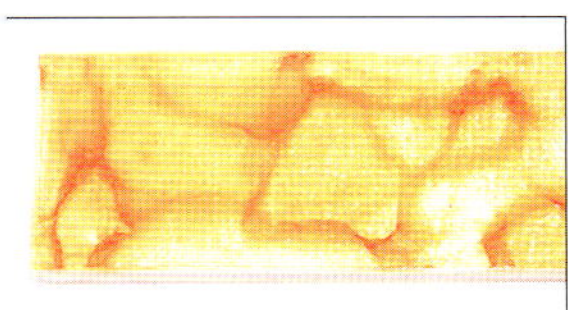

## Acrylic Desk Ruler

Surrounding your workspace with beautiful things reduces stress and makes you more efficient in your tasks. This ruler is the perfect gift for the work-aholic in your family.
1. Spritz a clear acrylic block ruler with Blending Solution. Apply drops of Alcohol Ink (re-inker) to the ruler while the Solution is wet. Let dry. • 2. Repeat if desired to achieve various mottled effects. Glue ribbon trim around the edges of the ruler.

Paperweight - page 13

Hope Magnet - page 13

Desk Ruler - page 13

## Faux Batik

*by Jen del Muro*

*Stampers and card makers love working with sumptuous papers. Now you can create beautiful background papers in soft, subtle tones and fun, cheerful main images by incorporating mulberry paper into your project. This porous paper creates excellent texture and appeal.*

*Fabulous Looks with Mulberry Paper and Metal*

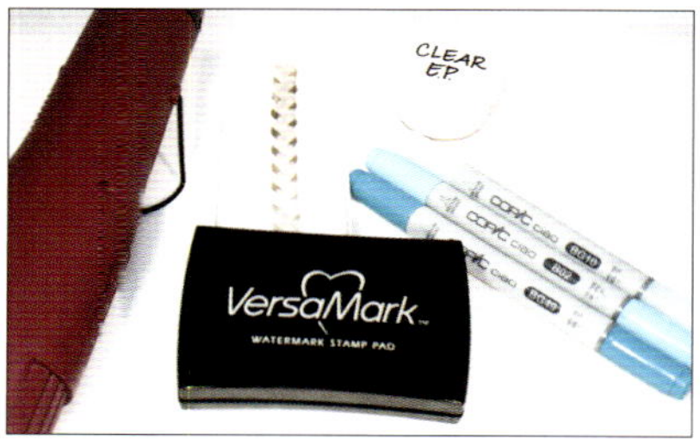

Here's an exciting use for mulberry paper. You'll love the wonderful color variations.

Stamp a random design on mulberry paper with embossing ink. Emboss with Clear embossing powder.

Color the non-embossed areas using alcohol based markers. Spritz with alcohol to make the ink color bleed.

See page 14 for materials and instructions.

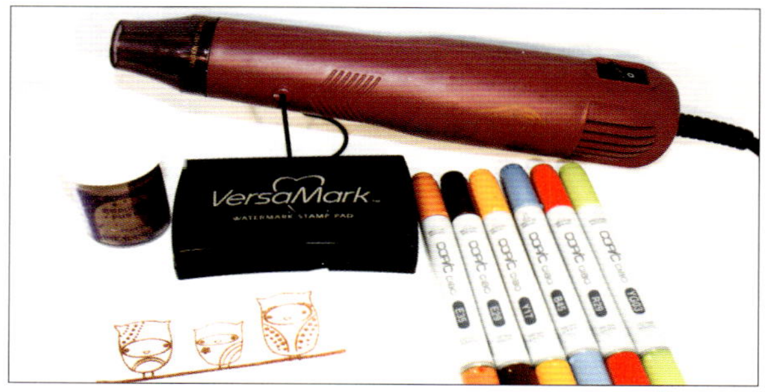


Gorgeous embossing makes the Hoot Hoot Hooray card sparkle.

Stamp owls on Blue mulberry paper. Sprinkle with metallic embossing powder. Emboss.

Color the owls with markers as desired.

See page 14 for materials and instructions.

Mermaid
page 14

Hoot Hoot Hooray
page 14

page 3

by Barbara Buechley

## Coffee Filter Cards and Votive Candle Holder

SIZE: Cards: 5 1/4" x 7 1/2"
4 1/4" x 9 1/2"
Votive: 2" diameter, 2 3/4" tall

MATERIALS:
Cardstock or Glass votive candle holder
8" round coffee filters with fluted edges
*Sharpie* Permanent Markers
*Ranger* Blending Solution
Mister or spray bottle
*Scribbles* Gold paint
Matte Medium

INSTRUCTIONS:
1. Follow instructions on page 3 to color the filters.
2. Cut and fold cardstock to desired size.
3. Apply Matte Medium to the back of a decorated filter. Adhere it to a plain card, cardstock, or votive. Allow wrinkles to naturally occur.
4. Apply a coat of Matte Medium to the front of the filter for protection. Let dry.
Note: Decorated filters can be adhered with Matte Medium because the colors only bleed with alcohol.

page 4

by Jen del Muro

## Ice Cream Cone Card

*Celebrate every birthday with a fun card. Dyed embellishments complement the paper choices perfectly.*

SIZE: 4 1/4" x 5 1/2"

MATERIALS:
Cardstock
Decorative paper
Alcohol markers
Embellishments
Stamps *(Taylored Expressions)*
*Tsukineko* Brilliance Graphite Black ink
Punches
Dimensional Glue Dots

INSTRUCTIONS:
1. Mat and adhere decorative paper to card base.
2. Attach sentiment and scalloped edge panels.
3. Stamp image and color as desired; mat and mount on card base with dimensional glue dots.
4. Color embellishments (flowers, buttons, ribbon) and attach to card when dry.

## Goody Bag

*Fill a bag with treats and love from your kitchen. Dyed ribbons and buttons add that special finishing touch to the label.*

SIZE: 3 1/2" x 6"

MATERIALS:
Goody bag
*Copic* Alcohol Markers
*Ranger* Blending Solution
Mister or spray bottle

INSTRUCTIONS:
Print or write label. Color the flower, buttons and ribbon with markers. Mist lightly with Blending solution. Let dry. Attach to bag.

## I Ruff You Card

*Design a delightful card for the dog lover in your family. The pink ribbon is resting upon a dyed metal clip...very cool!*

SIZE: 4 1/4" x 5 1/2"

MATERIALS:
Cardstock
Decorative paper
*Copic* Alcohol Markers
Embellishments
Stamps *(The Cat's Pajamas)*
*Tsukineko* Brilliance Graphite Black ink
Punches
Sewing machine
Dimensional Glue Dots

INSTRUCTIONS:
1. Mat and adhere paper to card.
2. Mat, stitch and attach Light Pink panel.
3. Stamp image and color as desired; mat and mount on card. Stamp sentiment and attach to card.
4. Color embellishments (metal clip, ribbon, rhinestone), attach to card when dry.

## Trick Or Sweet

*Send a ghostly greeting this Halloween filled with spooky wishes for a howling good time.*

SIZE: 4 1/4" x 5 1/2"

MATERIALS:
Cardstock
Decorative paper
*Copic* Alcohol Markers
Embellishments
Stamps *(Taylored Expressions)*
*Tsukineko* Brilliance Graphite Black ink
Scallop square die cut
Dimensional Glue Dots

INSTRUCTIONS:
1. Mat paper, scallop edge and sentiment

...Trick or Sweet continued

panels. Tie twill around and then attach to card base.
2. Stamp image and color as desired; mat and mount on card.
3. Attach brads and embellishments to card.

page 5

by Jen del Muro

## Hey Sweetie

*I'm thinking of you and hope you have a day filled with sweetness and light.*

SIZE: 4 1/4" x 5 1/2"

MATERIALS:
Cardstock
Embossed paper
*Copic* Alcohol Markers
Embellishments
Stamps *(My Favorite Things)*
*Tsukineko inks* (Brilliance Graphite Black, VersaMark)
Die cut heart
White embossing powder
Dimensional Glue Dots

INSTRUCTIONS:
1. Mat and adhere embossed panel to card.
2. Stamp image on heart die cut. Color as desired. Emboss sprinkles. Adhere to card.
3. Stamp sentiment panel, mat and attach to card.
4. Color brads with alcohol markers to match card and attach. Tie bow and attach to card.

## Thank You Fairy Much

*Many thanks are winging their way to your door. Check out the dyed acrylic star and paper flower.*

SIZE: 4 1/4" x 5 1/2"

MATERIALS:
Cardstock, Embossed paper
*Copic* Alcohol Markers
Mister
Blending Solution or Rubbing Alcohol
Embellishments
Stamps *(Stamping Bella)*
*Tsukineko* Brilliance Graphite Black ink
Dimensional Glue Dots

INSTRUCTIONS:
1. Adhere Light Green panel to card. Mat and adhere embossed paper.
2. Stamp image and color as desired; mat and mount on card base with dimensional glue dots. Stamp sentiment panel and attach to card.
3. Color acrylic star. Mist with rubbing alcohol. Let dry and attach along with other embellishments.

page 5
by Jen del Muro

## Have a Fairy Christmas

*You don't have to believe in fairies to create your own bit of magic with blended colors.*

SIZE: $4^1/_4$" x $5^1/_2$"

MATERIALS:
Cardstock
Decorative paper
*Copic* Alcohol Markers
Embellishments
Stamps *(The Cat's Pajamas)*
*Tsukineko* Brilliance Graphite Black ink
Punches
Dimensional Glue Dots

INSTRUCTIONS:
1. Mat Dark Green and decorative paper. Tie twill around and then attach to card. Attach scallop edge and Dark Green seam strip.
2. Stamp image and color as desired; mat and mount on card.
3. Stamp sentiment panel. Mat and attach to card base.
4. Color brads with alcohol markers to match card. Let dry and attach.

## 29th Again

*It doesn't matter how many times you turn 29. Celebrate!*

SIZE: 5" x 5"

MATERIALS:
Cardstock
Decorative paper
*Copic* Alcohol Markers
Embellishments
Stamps *(The Cat's Pajamas)*
*Tsukineko* Brilliance Graphite Black ink
Dimensional Glue Dots

INSTRUCTIONS:
1. Mat and attach decorative paper to card.
2. Stamp sentiment panel, mat and adhere.
3. Stamp penguin and gift images and color as desired. Mat and attach to card.
4. Color embellishments (flower and button) to match. Let dry and attach to card.

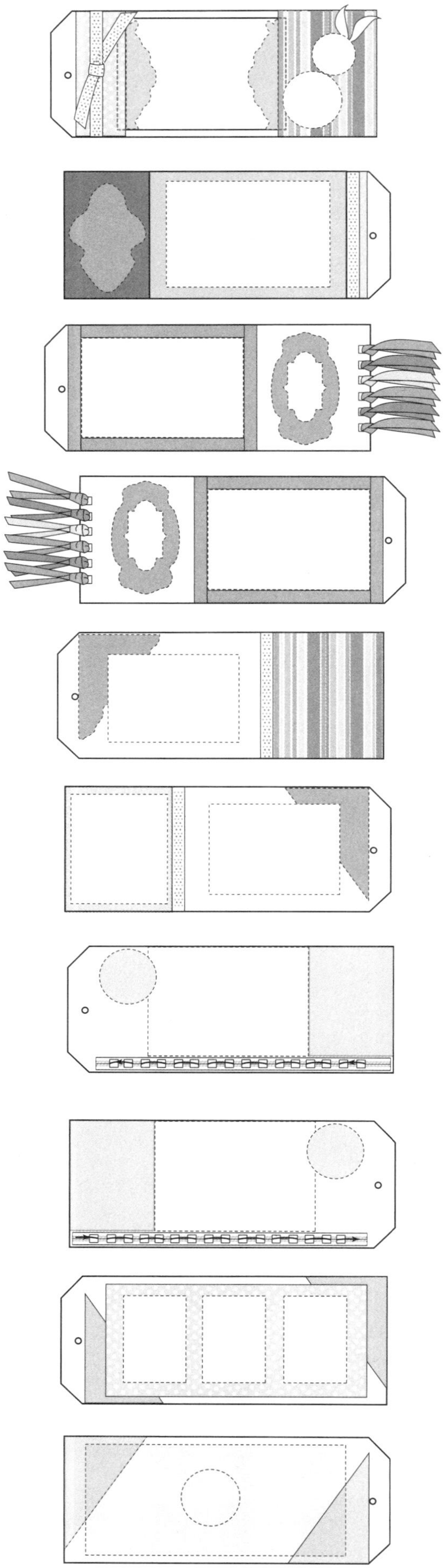

page 6
by Paula Phillips

## Clear Acrylic Album

SIZE: 4" x 10"

MATERIALS:
*AccuCut* 5 Clear 4" x 10" tag shaped album pages
$1^1/_4$" binder ring
*American Crafts* 2-sided cardstock papers
*Ranger* Alcohol Inks
*Hambly* printed transparency sheet
*American Crafts* layered self-adhesive felt embellishments (Details)
Ribbon
*Zutter Bind it All!* Binding Machine
*Ranger* Glossy Accents
Glue Dots
Photos:
- 6 - $3^1/_2$" x 5"
- 2 – $2^3/_4$" x 4"
- 1 – $3^1/_2$" x 3"
- 3 – $2^3/_4$" x 2"

Paper Cutting Dimensions:
- Green dot paper with Blue back: $1^1/_2$" x $3^3/_4$"; $3^1/_2$" x 8"
- Stripe paper with Red back: 3" x 4"; $3^1/_2$" x 4"
- Butterfly paper with Red back: 4" x 6"

INSTRUCTIONS:
Remove film from both sides of each page.
Page 1: On the backside of the cover, glue a $3^1/_2$" x 5" photo so it shows through on the front. Cut out pieces of the transparency and adhere to front of page to frame photo. Adhere papers and embellishments to page.
Adhere photo and transparency shape to back of page.
Page 2: Use the binding machine to punch holes in the end of the page that does not have the hole punched already. Tie ribbons through the holes. • Make a ribbon frame to fit your photo. Ink the edges of a transparency design and adhere to the right of the ribbon frame. • Adhere photos inside the ribbon frame both on the front and the back sides.
Page 3: Glue paper and ribbon to the outer edge on both sides of the page. Adhere a transparency design in the upper inside corner. Adhere a photo to the front and back of the page.
Page 4: Use the binding machine to punch holes along the bottom edge of the page. Weave ribbon through the holes. Adhere transparency design. Adhere photo and embellishment to both sides of the page.
Page 5: Adhere transparency design to the corners of the page. Adhere papers and photos. Adhere circle transparency design on the back of the page.
Assembly: Insert the ring through the hole in each page and tie ribbons onto the ring.

page 7

by Paula Phillips

**Perpetual Calendar**

SIZE: 12" x 12"

MATERIALS:

*Petersen Arne* 12" x 12" Acrylic calendar
*Ranger* (Blending Solution; Alcohol inks: Wild Plum, Lettuce, Stream, Butterscotch; Glossy Accents)
Self-adhesive crystal designs
Embellishments (Flowers, Brads, Ribbon)
Painter's tape or masking tape
Paintbrush, Cotton balls , Glue Dots

INSTRUCTIONS:

1. On back of the calendar, tape off the center of the calendar and a space in the top right in which the month will be written.
2. Dab on alcohol inks one color at a time. Repeat with several colors. Let dry.
3. Seal by brushing Glossy Accents over the alcohol inks. Let dry. Remove tape.
4. Adhere embellishments as desired.

**Clear Acrylic Card**

SIZE: 4¼" x 5½"

MATERIALS:

4¼" x 5½" Clear Acrylic folded card "
*Hambly* printed Transparency sheet (use a 2½" x 3½" section)
*Ranger* Alcohol Inks, Blending Solution and Glossy Accents
*American Crafts* 2-sided 4¼" x 5½" cardstock paper, 'Details' felt accent, and 9" of ¼" Ribbon for a bow

INSTRUCTIONS:

1. Use a cotton ball or applicator to dab colors of Alcohol Ink onto the back of a clear Screen Print Transparency. Let dry.
2. Cut out a 2½" x 3½" Transparency section and
adhere it to the front of the card with Glossy Accents. Let dry.
3. Adhere a felt embellishment and a ribbon bow to the card front.
4. Adhere cardstock inside the back of card.

page 8

by Jen del Muro

**Never Grow Up**

SIZE: 4¼" x 5½"

MATERIALS:

Cardstock, Embossed paper
*Copic* Alcohol Markers, Mister

...Never Grow Up continued

Blending Solution or Rubbing Alcohol
Embellishments
Stamps *(Stamping Bella)*
*Tsukineko* Brilliance Graphite Black ink
Dimensional Glue Dots

INSTRUCTIONS:

1. Mat and adhere papers to card.
2. Stamp image and color as desired; mat and mount on card. Stamp sentiment and adhere to card.
3. Color acrylic flower. Mist with rubbing alcohol. Let dry and attach along with other embellishments.

**Dance, Sing, Live Tag Card**

SIZE: 4¼" x 5½"

MATERIALS:

Acrylic tag 1⅝" x 3¼"
Cardstock, Embossed paper
*Copic* Alcohol Markers, Mister
Blending Solution or Rubbing Alcohol
Embellishments
Stamps *(Verve Stamps)*
*Tsukineko* ink pads (StazOn, VersaMark)
Clear embossing powder
Heat gun, Sewing machine
Dimensional Glue Dots

INSTRUCTIONS:

Tag: 1. Color back of tag with markers.
2. Spritz with alcohol. Let dry.
3. Color the sheer ribbon with the same Purple used on the tag.
4. Stamp tag front with StazOn ink and attach ribbons.

Card: 1. Mat dry embossed Red panel and adhere to card.
2. Stamp flower with VersaMark and heat emboss with Clear embossing powder. Attach this panel to card.
3. Mat and stitch White panel. Adhere to card.
4. Adhere tag with a glue dot behind the ribbon.

page 9

by Jen del Muro

**Acrylic Desk Ruler**

SIZE: 2" x 8"

MATERIALS:

*Apple Pie Memories* 2" x 8" Acrylic block ruler
Decorative paper (cut 3" x 3", score in ½" on each side and cut out corners)
*Copic* Reinker bottles with Alcohol Ink
Mister
Blending Solution or Rubbing Alcohol
Embellishments (Ribbon, Charm)
Double-sided tape, Hot glue gun

INSTRUCTIONS:

1. On bottom side of acrylic block, spray rubbing alcohol and apply drops of alcohol ink. Allow to dry.

...Acrylic Desk Ruler continued

2. Spritz with rubbing alcohol and allow to dry. Repeat if desired to achieve various mottled effects.
3. Attach decorative paper to block.
4. Cover side edge of paper with ribbon.
5. Attach bow and butterfly charm.

**Hope Magnet**

SIZE: 2" x 2"

MATERIALS:

*Apple Pie Memories* 2" x 2" acrylic block
White cardstock (cut to 3" x 3" and scored in ½" on each side, with corners cut out)
*Copic* Alcohol Markers, Mister
Blending Solution or Rubbing Alcohol
Stamp *(Verve Stamps)*
*Tsukineko* Brilliance Graphite Black ink
Twill ribbon
Double-sided tape, Hot glue gun

INSTRUCTIONS:

1. On bottom side of acrylic block, color stripes with markers.
2. Spritz with alcohol and allow to dry.
3. Stamp verse on cardstock and tape to block, folding up the edges.
4. Cover paper side edges by attaching twill with double-sided tape.
5. Apply second layer of ribbon around sides and attach bow to top.
6. Hot glue a magnet on the back.

**Acrylic Paperweight**

*Acrylic pieces are a fun and easy way to dress up any project. With alcohol markers, you can simply color them to match. Spritz a little rubbing alcohol on the colored acrylic pieces and watch them come to life!*

SIZE: 3" x 3"

MATERIALS:

*Apple Pie Memories* 3" x 3" acrylic block
White cardstock (cut 4" x 4", score in ½" on each side and cut out corners)
*Copic* Alcohol Markers, Mister
Blending Solution or Rubbing Alcohol
Photo, Twill ribbon, Rhinestones
Double-sided tape

INSTRUCTIONS:

1. On bottom side of acrylic block, color dots with markers.
2. Spritz with alcohol and allow to dry.
3. Attach photo to cardstock. Tape cardstock to block, folding up the edges.
4. Cover paper side edges by taping twill in place.
5. Apply rhinestones around sides for a finishing touch.

page 10
by Jen del Muro

**Mermaid Card**

SIZE: $4^1/4$" x $5^1/2$"

MATERIALS:
Cardstock, Mulberry paper
*Copic* Alcohol Markers
Mister
Blending Solution or Rubbing Alcohol
Embellishments
Silver cording
Corner punch
Stamps *(My Favorite Things)*
*Tsukineko* inks (Brilliance Graphite Black, VersaMark ink)
Clear embossing powder
Sewing machine
Heat gun
Dimensional Glue Dots

INSTRUCTIONS:
1. Emboss mulberry paper with Clear embossing powder and color in non-embossed areas using alcohol based markers.
2. Spritz colored mulberry paper with alcohol so the ink spreads between embossed areas. Let dry. Sew onto Dark Green panel and adhere to card.
3. Attach Dark Green with Black mat panel to card and tie Silver cording with colored charm.
4. Stamp and color image. Mat with Dark Green and Black cardstock. Punch corners and attach brads. Adhere panel to card at an angle.

**Hoot Hoot Hooray**

SIZE: $4^1/4$" x $5^1/2$"

MATERIALS:
Cardstock
*Copic* Alcohol Markers
Stamps *(My Favorite Things)*
*Tsukineko* VersaMark ink
Bronze embossing powder
Dimensional Glue Dots

INSTRUCTIONS:
1. Emboss image on mulberry paper with Bronze embossing powder and color as desired.
2. Adhere to White cardstock matted with Dark brown cardstock.
3. Stamp sentiment and adhere matted squares to card.
4. Mount main image panel on top.

page 20
by Paula Phillips

**It's a Boy Card**

SIZE: $4^1/4$" x $5^1/2$"

MATERIALS:
*Ranger* $4^1/4$" x $5^1/2$" White Glossy cardstock
*Sizzix* (die cut machine; dies: Lollipop alphabet, dog)
Blue ribbon
1 Blue gem $^1/4$"
4 Yellow gems $^1/4$"
Two 1" Blue paper squares
*Ranger* (Blending Solution; Clear Stickles; Alcohol inks: Stream, Butterscotch)
Cotton balls or alcohol ink applicator
Scallop edge scissors
Paper piercing tool
*Xyron* (machine, repositionable adhesive)
Tape runner
Liquid adhesive

INSTRUCTIONS:
1. Die cut the letters "IT'S A BOY" and the dog from extra glossy paper.
2. Run the die cuts through the *Xyron* machine and adhere them to the center front of the glossy card.
3. Drip Butterscotch alcohol ink and several drops of Blending Solution onto a cotton ball. Rub in a circular motion over the top of the card. Repeat with Stream ink. The more Blending Solution you use, the lighter the ink color will be. Let dry.
4. Carefully remove the letters and puppy.
5. Apply Stickles over the White areas left from the paper "masks". Let dry completely. (If the paper buckles from the stickles, wait until it is dry, then place the paper face down onto a piece of wax paper and cover with another regular paper. Gently iron on a low setting to flatten the paper. Check often as you do this.
6. Cut each Blue square in half diagonally and adhere a triangle in each corner of the card.
7. Glue a Yellow gem in the center of each Blue triangle.
8. Glue the Blue gem for the dog's eye.
9. Use the paper piercing tool to make holes in each side of the dog's neck. Insert ribbon through the holes and tie in a bow on the front of the card.

**Friend Card**

SIZE: $4^1/4$" x $5^1/2$"

MATERIALS:
*Ranger* $4^1/4$" x $5^1/2$" White Glossy cardstock
*Ranger* (Blending Solution; Alcohol Inks: Butterscotch, Stream, Lettuce, Cranberry)
Cotton balls or alcohol ink applicator
Rub-on "stitches" or "sketches"
"Friend" rub-on word and definition
Paper flowers (1 Cranberry, 1 Sage Green) Brown brads (one $^1/4$", one $^3/8$")
Paper piercer, Painter's tape

INSTRUCTIONS:
1. Cut tape into 5 strips $^1/2$" x $5^1/2$".
2. Place the tape strips on card front to mask areas while the card is inked.
3. Drip alcohol ink and several drops of Blending Solution on a cotton ball. Rub over the card in a circular motion. The Blending Solution lightens the inks and increases the blend on the glossy paper.
4. Repeat with colors of Alcohol Ink. Let dry.
5. Remove the painter's tape carefully.
6. Using the same inking technique as above, ink over the entire front of the card with Butterscotch ink only. Let dry.
7. Apply rub-ons to card.
8. Use the paper piercing tool to make holes for the brads and attach flowers to the card.

page 19
by Suzanne McNeill

**Metal Swirls Card**

*It looks like antique embossed tin but it's light as a feather! You're going to love this inexpensive, easy technique.*

SIZE: $4^1/4$" x $5^1/2$"

MATERIALS:
Heavy duty aluminum foil
$4^1/4$" x $5^1/2$" Black card
4" x 5" cardboard
*Copic* Alcohol Markers
Mister or spray bottle
*Ranger* Blending Solution
Dry embossing tool
*Stampabilities* Swirl stamp
*Tsukineko* Black StazOn ink
Clear flat-back rhinestones (two $^3/8$", forty $^3/16$")
*Beacon* The Ultimate! glue

INSTRUCTIONS:
1. Cover cardboard with foil. Glue foil to the back of the cardboard. Use an embossing tool to texturize the foil.
2. Beginning with the darkest color, color the foil with markers, blending the colors where they meet. Let dry. Mist lightly with Blending Solution. Let dry.
3. Stamp swirl with StazOn ink. Let dry.
4. Adhere decorated foil to front of card. Add rhinestones.

## Forever Love Metal Heart Card

SIZE: $4^1/_4$" x $5^1/_2$"

MATERIALS:

Heavy duty aluminum foil
$4^1/_4$" x $5^1/_2$" Red card
4" x 5" cardboard
3" x $3^1/_2$" cardboard heart
*Copic* Alcohol Markers
Mister or spray bottle
*Ranger* Blending Solution
Dry embossing tool
"Forever" stamp
*Tsukineko* Black StazOn ink
20" Rick rack $^1/_2$" wide
*Beacon* The Ultimate! glue

INSTRUCTIONS:

1. Glue cardboard heart to center of cardboard. Cover with foil. Use an embossing tool to press foil around the heart and to texturize the foil. Glue foil to the back of the cardboard.
2. Beginning with the darkest color, color the foil with markers, blending where the colors meet. Let dry. Mist lightly with Blending Solution. Let dry. Stamp "forever" with StazOn ink. Let dry.
3. Color rick rack with markers. Mist with Blending solution or alcohol to make the colors bleed. Let dry. Adhere rick rack to edge of card front.
4. Adhere decorated foil to front of card.

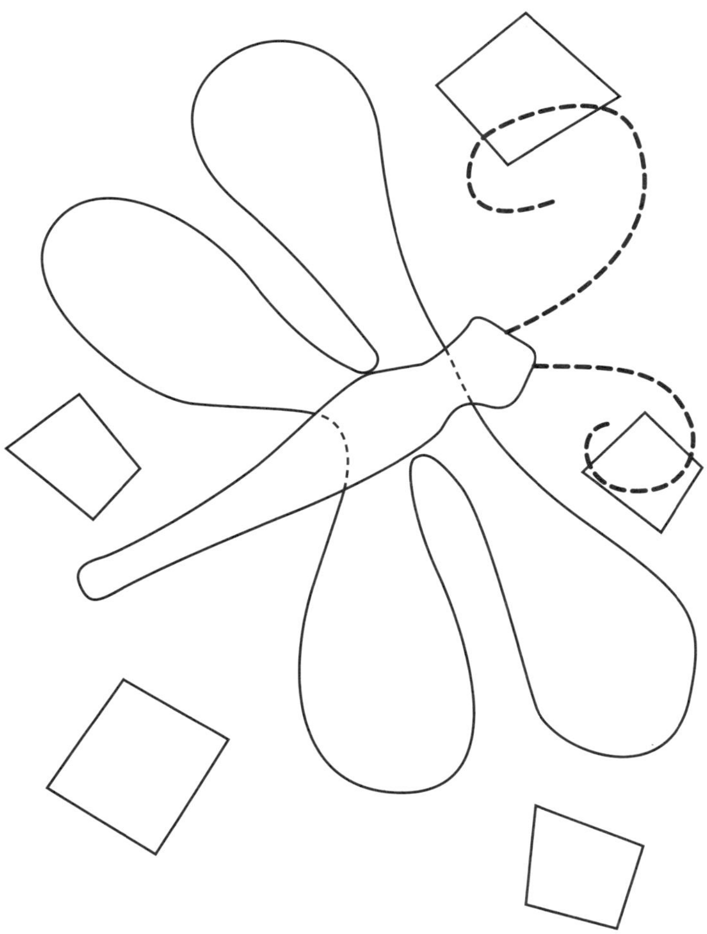

page 21

by Suzanne McNeill

## Stitched Collage Cards

patterns are on pages 15 and 16

SIZE: $4^1/_4$" x $5^1/_2$"

MATERIALS:

*Ranger* $4^1/_4$" x $5^1/_2$" White Glossy cardstock
Assorted colored and dyed coffee filter or fabric scraps
4" x 5" cardstock or decorative paper
*Ranger* Alcohol Inks in bottles
*Ranger* Blending Solution
Mister or spray bottle
Cotton balls
Sewing machine, thread
Embroidery floss
Glue stick

INSTRUCTIONS:

Dyed Fabric: Use any material for your collage: cotton, light wool, satin, sheer, silk, mulberry paper, coffee filters, ribbons, lace. Strive to create color variations and interesting patterns. Color the pieces with markers, spray with alcohol, and let dry. Press the pieces flat with a dry iron before using.

1. Spray front of card with Blending Solution. While wet, drip alcohol ink onto the surface. Smear ink with cotton ball. Let dry. Spray again and drip ink onto surface. Let these drips remain as texture. Let dry.
2. Cut fabric scraps using patterns. Glue pieces in place. Sew a Zig-zag or Running stitch around each shape. The antennae on the butterfly is handstitched with 6 strands of floss.
3. Adhere cardstock or paper to the inside cover of the card to hide the stitching.

flower pattern goes with
'Stitched Collage Cards' on page 15

page 22

by Suzanne McNeill

**Tie-Dye Cards**

SIZE: $4^1/4$" x $5^1/2$"

MATERIALS:

$4^1/4$" x $5^1/2$" card
Mulberry paper or coffee filters
Assorted papers and embellishments
*Sharpie or Copic* Alcohol markers
*Ranger* Blending Solution
Mister or spray bottle
Binder clips
Matte Medium by *Golden* or
Double-sided tape, or *Xyron* adhesive
Glue stick

INSTRUCTIONS:

Dyed paper: 1. Fold and pleat paper or coffee filter like an accordion. Secure the folds with binder clips.
2. Color around the edge of the binder clips on both sides of the paper with 1 or 2 colors of permanent markers as desired.
3. Spray well with Blending Solution to make the colors bleed through all layers.
4. Let dry. Remove binder clips and unfold to reveal the gorgeous design in the paper.
Card: Layer papers as desired. Adhere embellishments.

page 24

by Donna Goss

**Wish Banner**

SIZE: triangles: $5^1/2$" wide x 6" tall
banner: 6" x 33"

MATERIALS:

4 *Maya Road* 5½" x 6" chipboard banner triangles
3" x 8½" Aqua cardstock
3" x 8½" Flirty fully embossed print cardstock *(My Minds Eye)*
*Ranger* (2 pcs 6½" x 8½" Sticky-Back Canvas; Cranberry Adirondack ink pad; Tiara Stickles, Alcohol ink applicator, Solution; Cut n Dry foam; Acrylic paint dabbers: Cranberry, Aqua; Alcohol inks: Cranberry, Pearl)
Mister or spray bottle
2 yds Aqua ½" wide ribbon
*Prima* 4 Pink paper flowers
*Mark Richards* 4 Clear rhinestones
*Advantus Corp* 2 grungeboard birds; grundgeboard letters that spell WISH
*Stampers Anonymous* Swirl stamp
*Marvy Uchida* punches Mega regular oval, Giga scallop oval)
Kosher salt
Craft knife, Cutting mat, Scissors, Pencil

INSTRUCTIONS:

1. Trace triangle shapes on canvas. Apply Cranberry and Pearl alcohol inks to applicator and dab on canvas. Re-apply inks to applicator when needed to completely cover triangles. Spray Blending Solution heavily on canvas till puddles form. Sprinkle with salt. Let dry overnight. Wipe off salt and cut out triangles.
2. Paint chipboard triangles with Aqua dabber. Let dry.
3. Adhere canvas to chipboard triangles.
4. Cut holes for hanging.
5. Punch 4 scallop ovals from embossed cardstock. Punch 4 regular ovals from Aqua cardstock. Edge Aqua ovals using Cranberry ink.
6. Adhere Aqua ovals to scallops. Adhere scallop ovals to canvas triangles.
7. Paint letters with Cranberry dabber. Let dry. Attach to Aqua ovals. Apply Tiara stickles to letters. Let dry.
8. Adhere flowers to points of triangles. Adhere rhinestones to flower centers.
9. Thread ribbon through holes in triangles tying knots with loop at ends. Cut 5 ribbons 4" long. Tie between triangles.
10. Paint birds with Aqua dabber. Let dry.
11. Stamp swirls using Cranberry ink pad. Spread Stickles on birds using your finger. Let dry.
12. Adhere birds to knots at ends of ribbon.

**Pink Resist Bird Pin**

*I love the dyed tail feather and the quality of the finish details will have everyone inquiring of the boutique from which this pin was purchased.*

SIZE: 3" x $5^1/2$"

MATERIALS:

Chipboard bird *(Maya Road)*
*Copic* Alcohol markers (RV11 Pink, R59 Maroon)
*Ranger* (3¼" x 4" Sticky-Back Canvas; Blending Solution; Glossy Accents)
Mister bottle
*Mark Richards* Pearl rhinestones (1 large, 8 small)
*Impress Rubber Stamps* Damask stamp
White pigment ink pad
*Judi Kins* Detail White embossing powder
3¼" x 4" Black felt
*Ranger* Heat gun
Pin back, 2 White feathers, Glitter, Tweezers, Pencil, Scissors, Jewelry glue

...Pink Resist Bird Pin continued

INSTRUCTIONS:

1. Stamp Damask image several times on canvas using White ink pad, re-inking between impressions. Emboss with White powder. Let cool.
2. Color canvas using RV11 Pink marker. Highlight several areas of stamped images using R59 Maroon marker. Spray canvas with Blending Solution. Let dry.
3. Trace chipboard bird on canvas. Cut out on inside of pencil line. Edge canvas with R59 marker to finish edges. Color chipboard bird edges using R59 marker. Adhere canvas to chipboard.
4. Apply large pearl for eye on bird. Apply small pearls to body.
5. Color feathers with R59 marker. Adhere to back of chipboard bird. Glue back of chipboard to felt. Cut out around bird. Apply Glossy Accents over canvas bird and let dry. Adhere pin back to felt.

## Blue Bird Pin

*Special pins are a must-have in every accessory wardrobe. They also make wonderful gifts.*

SIZE: 3" x $4^{1}/2$"

MATERIALS:

*Maya Road* chipboard (bird, branch)
2" x 2" chipboard square
*Ranger* (Sticky-Back Canvas $2^{1}/2$ x 4"; Alcohol Ink applicator; Espresso acrylic paint dabber; Vintage Photo Distress Crackle paint; Blending Solution; Alcohol inks: Stream, Silver)
*My Minds Eye* Flirty cardstock (2" x 2" Fun Lovin' Spots, 1" x 2" Plain Joy)
Large Clear rhinestone *(Mark Richards)*
*Golden* (Asphalt glaze, Gel Medium)
Pin back
Scissors
Paper towel
Pencil
Paintbrush
Plastic cup
Jewelry adhesive

INSTRUCTIONS:

Branch: 1. Paint branch with Espresso dabber. Let dry.
2. Apply crackle paint. Let dry. Use a paper towel to rub Asphalt glaze into formed cracks. Rub off most of the glaze on top of the branch using a damp paper towel.
Wing: 3. Paint with Espresso dabber. Let dry. Trace wing on Joy cardstock and cut out. Adhere to wing.
Background Square: 4. Paint with Espresso dabber. Let dry.
5. Adhere Spots cardstock to square.
Bird: 6. Paint canvas with Gel Medium to seal. Let dry.

...bird with Branch Pin continued

7. Apply Stream and Silver alcohol inks and then Blending Solution to applicator. Dab on canvas. If needed, re-apply several times to cover canvas. Apply Blending Solution by itself to lighten the color. Let dry.
8. Using a paintbrush, draw circles on canvas with Blending Solution. Color edges of chipboard bird using alcohol ink left on applicator. When canvas is dry, trace chipboard bird on canvas. Cut out and adhere to chipboard bird.
9. Adhere rhinestone for bird's eye.
Assembly: 10. Adhere branch to square. Adhere bird on top of branch and square. Adhere wing to bird.
11. Glue pin back on back of square.

page 25

by Donna Goss

## Bird Bodice

*It's art for art's sake. Indulge your creative spirit with a bit of whimsy.*

SIZE: $3^{1}/2$" x 13" x $3^{1}/2$" deep

MATERIALS:

12" tall wooden bodice *(Glue Art & Paper Studio)*
*Ranger* (4" x 6½" Sticky-Back Canvas; Antique Pewter Distress Crackle paint; Blending Solution; Alcohol Ink Applicator; Acrylic paint dabbers: Aqua, Silver; Alcohol Inks: Pearl, Stream, Silver)
36" White tulle 6" wide
12" Silver 24ga wire
18" Aqua/Brown 3/8" wide ribbon
6" Silver string
Charms (Crown, Key, Bird)
*Prima* Pink paper flowers (4 lg, 3 sm)
*Mark Richards* rhinestones (4 lg Clear, 50 sm Clear, 18 sm Pink)
Scissors
Pencil
Adhesive

INSTRUCTIONS:

1. Paint bodice with Aqua dabber. Let dry.
2. Trace bodice part on canvas. Paint canvas with Silver dabber to seal. Let dry.
3. Brush on a medium coat of Antique Pewter crackle. Let dry; DO NOT heat with a heat gun to speed up drying.
4. Using alcohol inks over metallic crackle gives a different look than using paint to highlight cracks. Apply Stream and Pearl inks and Blending Solution to applicator and dab on canvas. Let dry.
5. Cut out bodice from canvas and adhere to front of wooden bodice.
6. Thread tulle on wire to make tutu. Secure on back of bodice by twisting wire ends together. Tie ribbon in a knot around bodice to hide wire. Attach a large flower

...Bird Bodice continued

over knot in back. Adhere large rhinestone to flower center.
7. Thread key charm on Silver string and tie in a bow. Adhere to tulle. Apply small Clear rhinestones randomly on tulle tutu. Adhere flowers to base of wooden bodice. Apply large rhinestones to flower centers.
8. Color crown and bird charms using Silver alcohol ink. Let dry. Apply small Pink rhinestones to crown. Glue crown to top of wooden bodice. Adhere bird to base of wooden bodice.

page 26

by Donna Goss

## Bird on a Branch Card

*Dimension, texture and sparkle combine in an eye-catching design.*

SIZE: $4^{1}/4$" x $5^{1}/2$"

MATERIALS:

4¼" x 5½" card
*My Minds Eye* Flirty cardstock (4¼" x 5½" Fully Embrace, 2" x 5½" Simple Bliss)
*Ranger* (Crystal Stickles; Sticky-Back Canvas: 2¼" x 3¼" & 1" x 3")
*Copic* Alcohol markers (RV11, RV19, R59, BG10, BG13, E47, E49)
5½" Aqua ribbon 3/8" wide
*Maya Road* chipboard (bird with wing, branch)
*Mark Richards* Pink rhinestones
2 White feathers
Scissors
Pencil
Pop Up Glue Dots
Adhesive

INSTRUCTIONS:

1. Adhere Bliss cardstock to card.
2. Adhere ribbon where two patterns meet on card. Trim ribbon ends even at edge of card.
3. Tip: When you cut out canvas shapes such as flowers and color with markers, rub the marker around the cut edges to finish them off. Trace bird and wing on canvas. Color and draw details using markers. Cut out and attach to chipboard. Color edges of both canvas and chipboard using marker. Adhere wing to bird.
4. Color feathers with markers and adhere to back of chipboard bird.
5. Color branch with markers. Adhere to card. Adhere bird to branch and card.
6. Freehand draw flowers on canvas with markers. Cut out and color cut edges. Adhere to branch.
7. Apply rhinestones to bird (eye) and flower centers. Apply Stickles to bird with your finger.

## Bird on a Wire Card

*These happy birds are singing their hearts out to bring you a note of cheer.*

SIZE: 4 1/4" x 5 1/2"

MATERIALS:
*My Minds Eye* Flirty cardstock (4¼" x 5½" Funny flowers, 2½" x 4" Plain Joy)
Cardstock (2⅝" x 4⅛" Aqua, 2¼" x 3¾" Maroon)
*Copic* Alcohol markers (RV19, RV11, RV04, BG13, Y17)
*Ranger* (2" x 3½" Sticky-Back Canvas; Glossy Accents)
*Mark Richards* Silver ball rhinestones
5" Aqua 1½" wide ribbon
*Inkadinkado* Birds stamp
*Tsukineko* Tuxedo Black Memento ink pad
Scissors, Southwest corner punch
Pop Up Glue Dots, Tape runner adhesive

INSTRUCTIONS:
1. Stamp birds on canvas in Black ink. Color birds with markers, being careful near the edges. You do not want ink to bleed outside the stamped lines.
2. Punch corners of canvas. Adhere canvas to Maroon cardstock.
3. Adhere Aqua cardstock to card. Adhere Joy cardstock to Aqua. Adhere Maroon cardstock to Joy cardstock.
4. Tie ribbon in a knot and adhere to card. Trim ends.
5. Apply Glossy Accents to birds. Let dry. Adhere Silver rhinestones to canvas corners.
Tip: If the markers bleed outside your stamped lines, clean it up with White paint and a brush.

page 27
by Donna Goss

## Smile Wall Hanging

*Smile! It's time to experience the joy of creativityl.*

SIZE: 4 1/2" x 9 1/2"

...Smile Wall Hanging continued

MATERIALS:
*Maya Road* 4½" x 8½" scallop chipboard rectangle, phrase rub-on, chipboard bird)
*My Minds Eye* Flirty cardstock (5" x 9" Fun Lovin' Spots, 3½" x 5 ¼" Picnic Blanket)
Cardstock (3¾" x 5½" Pink, 3¼" x 5" White)
*Ranger*(4½" x 6½" Sticky-Back Canvas; Blending Solution; Aqua acrylic paint dabber; Alcohol Ink applicator; Cut n Dry foam; Pink Stickles; Alcohol Inks: Cranberry, Pearl)
1 yd Maroon ⅝" ribbon
*Mark Richards* large Clear rhinestone
Cutting mat, Craft knife, Scissors
Sanding block
*Provo Craft* Swirl embossing folder
Die cut machine
*We R Memory Keepers* Crop-A-Dile
Pop Up Glue Dots, Adhesive, Pencil

INSTRUCTIONS:
Bird: 1. Run canvas in embossing folder thru die cut machine to apply swirl texture.
2. Apply Pearl and Cranberry alcohol inks to canvas. Add Blending Solution if needed.
3. Trace chipboard bird on canvas and cut out. Paint chipboard bird with Aqua dabber. Let dry.
4. Adhere canvas to chipboard bird. Add rhinestone as eye of bird.
Backing: 5. Paint scallop chipboard rectangle with Aqua dabber. Let dry.
6. Adhere Spots cardstock to rectangle. Trim around scallops using craft knife. Sand edges. Rub Cranberry ink on edges using Cut n Dry square.
7. Punch 2 holes in top of rectangle. Thread ribbon through holes and tie knots to secure for hanging.
8. Apply rub-on phrase to White cardstock. Rub Aqua dabber on edges. Add Pink Stickles to flower centers of phrase. Let dry. Adhere Pink cardstock to rectangle. Layer Blanket cardstock on top. Adhere White cardstock. Attach bird to rectangle.

## Wooden Frame

*Every photo deserves a unique frame. Make yours to complement your decor.*

SIZE: 6 1/2" x 8 1/2"

MATERIALS:
6 ½" x 8 ½" wooden frame with a 4" x 6" window
*My Minds Eye* 7" x 9" Flirty Wrapped Up Stripes cardstock
Cardstock (4" x 6" Tan, 4 pcs 1¼" x 1¼" Mauve)
*Copic* Alcohol markers (RV11, E31)
Mister or spray bottle
*Zig* Black waterproof marker
*Ranger* (4 pcs Sticky-Back canvas 1" x 1"; Blending Solution; Raspberry acrylic paint dabber; Crystal Stickles)
*Mark Richards* sm Silver ball rhinestones
*Inkadinkado* bird cage stamp
*Tsukineko* Versafine Onyx Black ink pad
Pencil
Craft knife
Cutting mat
Adhesive

INSTRUCTIONS:
1. Paint frame with Raspberry acrylic paint dabber. Let dry. Cover front of frame with cardstock. Trim even at edges and cut out window hole.
2. Using a pencil, draw a harlequin pattern on canvas squares. Color with markers. Spritz canvas with Blending Solution. Let dry.
3. Trace over pencil lines with Black waterproof marker.
4. Adhere canvas to Mauve squares and then to frame.
5. Apply Stickles to canvas with your finger. Attach rhinestones to canvas corners.
6. Stamp bird cage on Tan cardstock in Black ink. Insert in frame.

### Suppliers

Most craft and variety stores carry an excellent assortment of supplies. If you need something special, ask your local store to contact the following companies.

**Markers & Alcohol Inks**

SHARPIE MARKERS - CHISEL TIP
sanfordcorp.com

COPIC MARKERS and REFILL INKS
copicmarker.com

ALCOHOL INKS and BLENDING SOLUTION
rangerink.com

**Accessories**

CLEAR ALBUMS and CARDS TO DIE CUT
accucut.com

SCREEN PRINT OVERLAYS
hamblyscreenprints.com

CLEAR FILM and CARDS
grafixarts.com
heroarts.com

STAZ-ON, BRILLIANCE and VERSACRAFT INK PADS
tsukineko.com

GLOSSY ACCENTS, GLOSSY CARDSTOCK, STICKY BACK CANVAS
rangerink.com

CLEAR ACRYLIC STAMPING BLOCK
applepiememories.com

2-SIDED PAPERS, 'DETAILS, 'SLICK' MARKERS
americancrafts.com

MIST IT! MISTER SPRAY BOTTLE
inspiredcrafts.com

PIPETTE DROPPERS
d-originals.com

BIND IT ALL! BINDING MACHINE
binditall.com

MATTE MEDIUM
goldenpaints.com

CLEAR PERPETUAL CALENDAR
petersen-arne.com

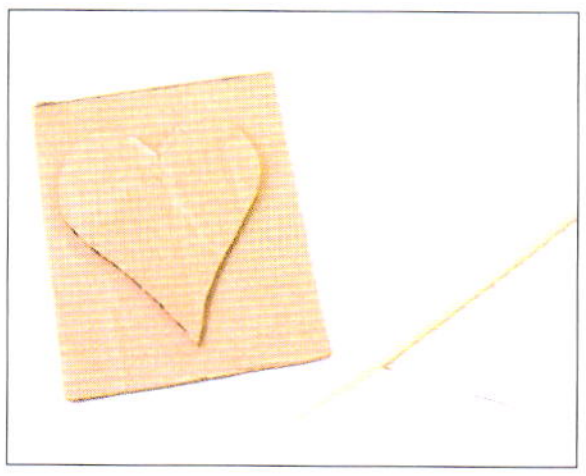

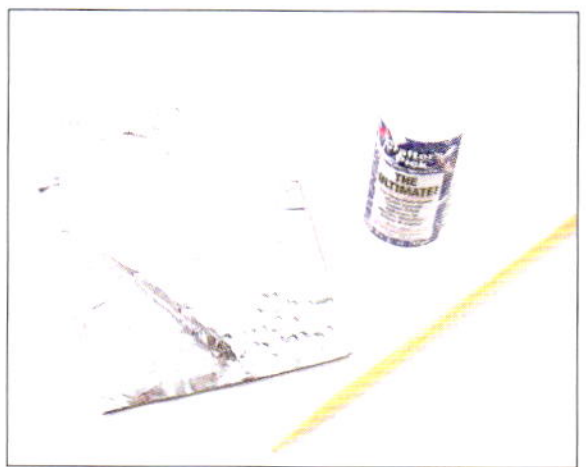

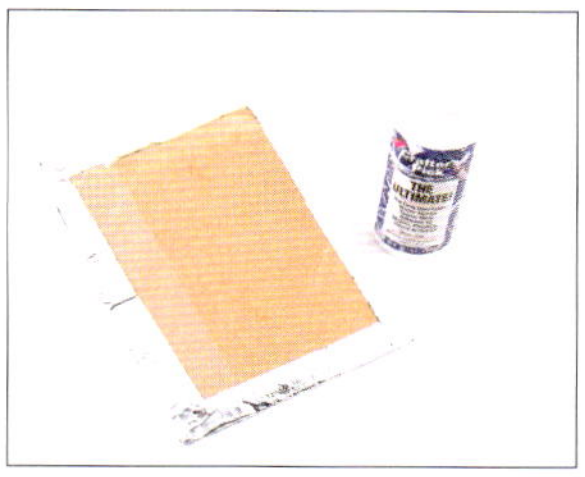

# Techniques with Metal and Glass

*by Suzanne McNeill*

*Metal and glass have a texture and shine unlike any other. Aluminum foil is inexpensive, easy to use, and readily available, so have fun with these techniques.*

**Little Metal Bucket -** Dab colors of Alcohol Ink onto metal. Add layers of color, beginning with the lightest. Let dry.

**Glass Votive Candle -** Dab colors of Alcohol Ink onto the surface of glass. Add layers of color, beginning with the lightest and working to the darkest. Allow texture to remain. Let dry.

**Metal Swirls Card -** Cover a 4″ x 5″ cardboard with aluminum foil. Beginning with the darkest color, color and blend foil with permanent markers. Let dry. Mist lightly with Blending Solution. Let dry. Stamp with Black StazOn ink. Let dry. Add embellishments.

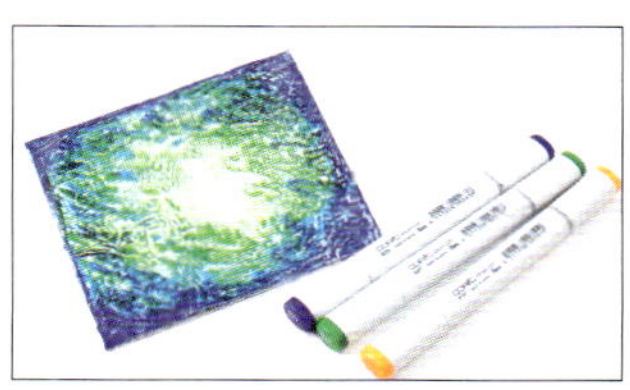

**Forever Love Card -** 1. Adhere a cardboard heart to a 4″ x 5″ cardboard. • 2. Cover with ***heavy duty*** aluminum foil (add a little glue to secure the design in place). Gently use an embossing tool or stick to press around the edges of the heart. • 3. Fold metal to the back of the cardboard and secure in place with glue. • 4. Use permanent markers to color the edge of the heart Red. • 5. Color the center of the heart Yellow, blending the colors where they touch. • 5. Leaving a margin around the heart, color the background Blue. • 6. Color the margin Green, blending where the colors touch. • 7. Lightly mist with Blending Solution to make the colors bleed just a bit. Let dry. • Glue the finished heart to the front of a $4\frac{1}{4}$" x $5\frac{1}{2}$" card.

**Colors of Copic Markers**
(over 200 colors available)

- Y17 Golden Yellow
- Y15 Cadmium Yellow
- Y26 Mustard
- YR04 Chrome Orange
- YR68 Orange
- YR09 Chinese Orange
- R24 Prawn
- R29 Lipstick Red
- RV29 Crimson
- R39 Garnet
- RV06 Cerise
- RV14 Begonia Pink
- RZZ Light Prawn
- RV17 Deep Magenta
- V04 Lilac
- V15 Mallow
- V17 Amethyst
- V09 Violet
- BV08 Blue Violet
- B12 Ice Blue
- B32 Pale Blue
- B34 Manganese
- B63 Light Hydrangea
- BG15 Aqua
- BG72 Ice Cream
- B24 Sky
- B29 Ultramarine
- B39 Prussian Blue
- BG93 Green Gray
- YG03 Yellow Green
- G24 Willow
- YG06 Yellowish Green
- G02 Spectrum Green
- BG13 Mint Green
- YG09 Lettuce Green
- G07 Nile Green
- G09 Veronese Green
- G17 Forest Green
- G28 Ocean Green
- R02 Flesh
- E04 Lipstick Natural
- E37 Sepia
- E09 Burnt Sienna
- E29 Burnt Umber
- B678 Bronze
- BV29 Slate
- Black

Friend - page 14

It's a Boy - page 14

## Techniques with Glossy Paper

*by Paula Phillips*

*If you have ever allowed your hand to glide over polished marble, you will appreciate the smooth texture of glossy paper. This shiny surface makes it easy to blend colors because it absorbs much differently from cardstock and other papers. I hope you enjoy this project as much as I have.*

### Coloring with Alcohol Inks

1. Tape strips of painter's tape or masking tape to a card front to mask the areas. Drip Alcohol Ink and several drops of Blending Solution onto a cotton ball. Rub color over the card in a circular motion. The Blending Solution lightens the inks and makes them blend more on the glossy paper. The more blending solution you use, the lighter the color will be. Repeat with additional colors of Alcohol Ink. Let dry. • 2. Remove the painter's tape carefully. • 3. Drip Butterscotch alcohol ink and several drops of Blending Solution onto a fresh cotton ball. Rub ink over the entire front of the card. Let dry. • 4. Apply rub-on 'stitches' along the edges of the front of the card. Apply the rub-on 'word and definition' in the corner. Use a paper piercing tool to make holes for the brads and attach flowers to the card.

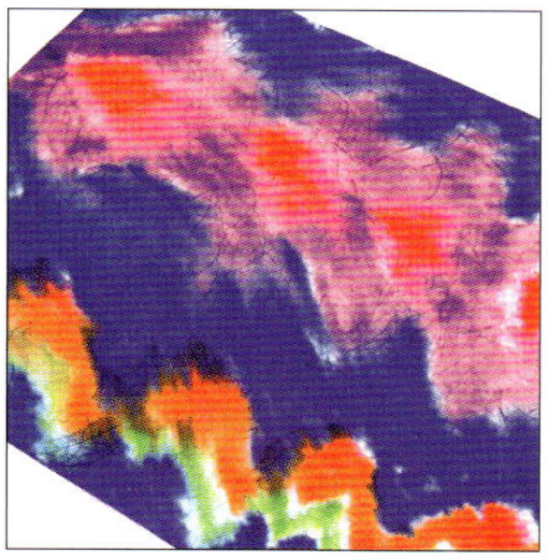

Butterfly - page 15

Strips of Color - page 15

Bright Flower - page 15

# Collage and Stitch Cards

*by Suzanne McNeill*

*Not only are these cards unique and beautiful, they are fun to make and a joy to receive. Create a variety of colorful backgrounds and simple designs for the collage elements.*

*Everybody is going to want one of these cards.*

SIZE: each card is 4 1/4" x 5 1/2" (fold 8 1/2" x 5 1/2" glossy cardstock in half)

**Glossy Cardstock Background -** 1. Spray glossy cardstock with Blending Solution. While wet, drip colors of Alcohol Ink onto the surface. Smear ink with a cotton ball. Let dry. • 2. Spray again and drip more ink on the surface. Let these drips remain as texture. Let dry.

**Collage Papers and Fabric -** 3. Dye mulberry paper, coffee filters, fabrics, ribbons, lace or China Silk to use as collage elements (page 3). Create variations of color on each piece. • 4. Cut out a variety of collage pieces and secure to the glossy cardstock with a glue stick. • 5. Stitch over the edges and areas of the collage pieces in a loose free form manner to secure them on the glossy cardstock. Pull threads to the back of the card and tie off. • 6. Glue color cardstock over the inside of the card to hide the stitching.

## Color Collage Papers and China Silk Fabric

Use permanent markers or Alcohol Inks, and Blending Solution or alcohol to color an assortment of mulberry papers, coffee filters and China Silk.

Make a collection of lights and darks - Reds, Oranges, Pinks, Purples, Blues and Greens to use for collage and stitched collage.

## Colors of Alcohol Inks by Ranger

### Metallic Colors

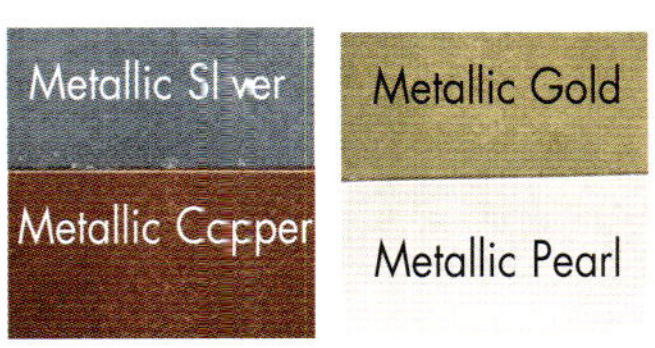

Tie-Dye Squares page 16

Tie-Dye Butterfly - page 16

Hi - page 16

# Tie-Dye Papers

*by Suzanne McNeill*

*Mulberry paper and coffee filters are a favorite of mine because of their great textures and versatility. They are soft, pliable, and strong.*

*You'll love the great looks with this fun technique. Add unique color patterns with markers to create wonderful backgrounds for cards.*

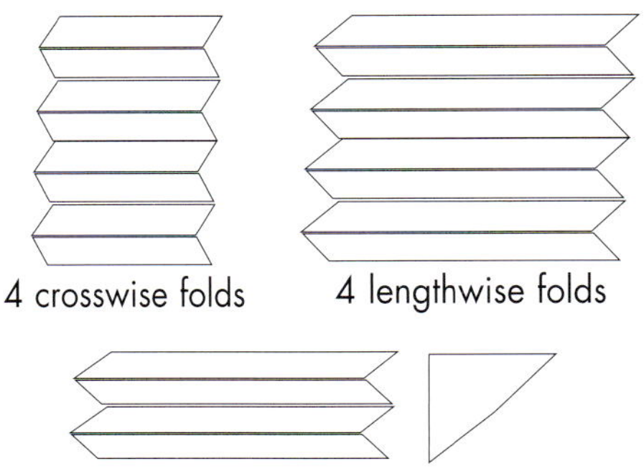

4 crosswise folds

4 lengthwise folds

2 lengthwise folds then a triangular corner

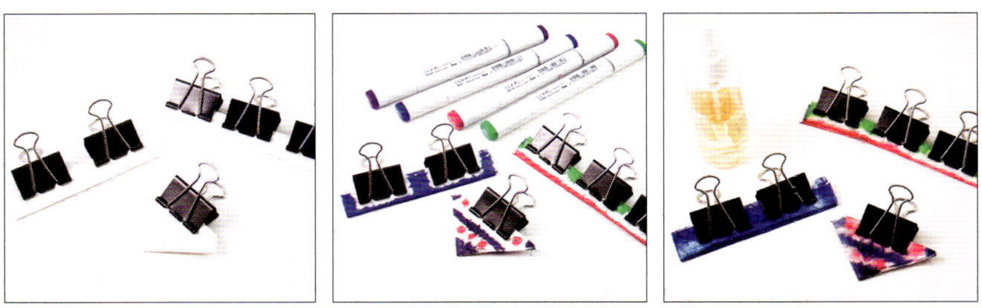

**Fold, Clip and Dye -** 1. Fold and pleat a piece of 4" x 5" mulberry paper or a coffee filter like an accordion (either crosswise with 2 clips, lengthwise with 3 clips, or triangular with 1 clip). Secure the folds with binder clips. • 2. Color around the edges of the binder clips on both sides of the paper with 1 or 2 colors of permanent markers as desired. • 3. Spray well with Blending Solution to make the colors bleed and run through all layers. • 4. Let dry. Remove binder clips and unfold to reveal the beautiful patterns and colors.
TIP: Secure dyed papers to chipboard or cardstock with matte medium, two-sided tape or Xyron adhesive.

Birds in the Forest

# Birds in the Forest

*by Suzanne McNeill*

*Begin a gallery of wonderful art with this small project. Color, dye, emboss, stamp and 'white wash' the background surface for interesting texture in the background, then add Glossy Accents for a special sparkle on the birds.*

SIZE: 7" x 20"

Materials - Four Color 5" x 7" stretched canvas panels • 6 small hinges • Alcohol Inks, Blending Solution, Glossy Accents, Embossing Ink and Powder from *Ranger* • Birds Stamp from *Martha Stewart by E.K.Success* • Swirls stamp from *Stampabilities* • StazOn ink from *Tsukineko* • White acrylic paint, Matte Medium from *Golden* • paintbrush.

Decorate 5" x 7" stretched canvas panels. Make 4 canvases and secure them together with small hinges in an accordion fashion.

**Shabby Distressed Look -** 1. Stamp a swirly design on canvas with embossing ink. Apply embossing powder, then pour off the excess. Emboss the swirly design with a heat gun. • 2. Spray canvas with Blending Solution. Drip ink colors on the wet surface. • 3. Spray on more Blending Solution and smear with a cotton ball. Let dry.• 4. Stamp birds on Sticky-back canvas with Black StazOn ink from *Tsukineko*. Let dry. • 5. Color bird images with permanent markers as desired. Let dry. Use scissors to cut colored bird shapes out of Sticky-Back canvas.

6. Stamp the swirly design on canvas with Black StazOn ink. Leave the stamped image a bit rough to give the background a distressed look. Let dry. • 7. Adhere birds and leaves to canvas. Coat the top of the birds with Matte Medium. Be sure the birds lay flat. Let dry. • 8. Mix Matte Medium with a few drops of White acrylic paint. Paint over the entire canvas. • 9. While the White paint is still wet, use a paper towel to wipe color off the birds. Also wipe some color off the background to give a distressed look. Let dry. • 10. Paint Matte Medium over the surface to add a bit of gloss. Let dry. Add puddles of Glossy Accents over all birds and leaves to add a sparkle texture. Allow to dry.

# Colors on Sticky-Back Canvas

*by Donna Goss*

*Indulge your creative spirit with a bit of whimsy. You'll love the wonderful ways to add texture, color and designs with Markers and Alcohol Inks.*

*Sticky-Back Canvas is a wonderful surface to embellish. It is so versatile, comes with its own adhesive, is easy to use, accepts colors beautifully and sticks to almost anything.*

*You'll love working with these exciting textures and colors.*

'Wish' Banner - page 16

## *Clever Banners, Brooches and Pins*

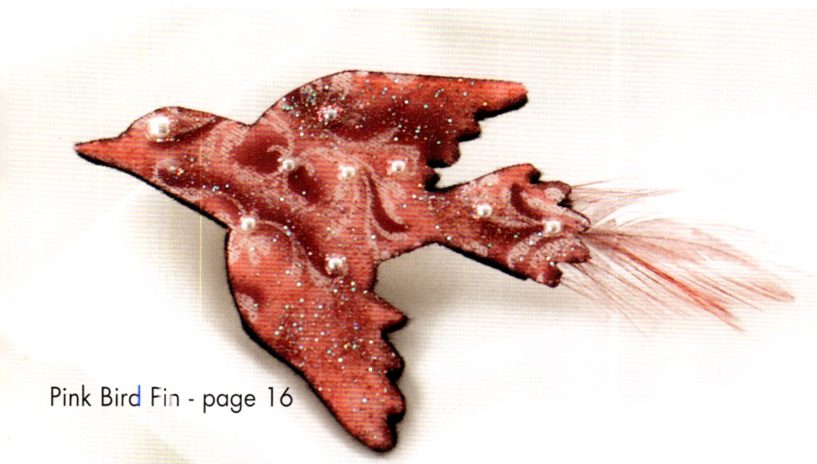

Pink Bird Pin - page 16

Blue Bird Pin - page 16

*You'll love these fabulous and easy textures on Sticky-Back Canvas. Pins are a must-have for every accessory wardrobe. They also make wonderful gifts.*

*Fabulous Looks with Sticky Canvas... on Everything*

Bodice - page 17

**Pink Bird Pin**

*Create special texture with beautiful swirls.*

1. Rubber stamp a 'damask' image several times on Sticky-Back Canvas using a White embossing ink pad and re-inking between impressions. Emboss with White embossing powder and a heat gun. Let cool.
2. Color canvas with a Pink marker from *Copic*. Highlight areas of the stamped images with a Maroon marker. Spray canvas with Blending Solution to blend and swirl the colors. Let dry.

**Blue Bird Pin**

*Mottled spots of color create a great look for this dainty bird.*

1. Apply Stream and Silver Alcohol Inks from *Ranger*. Apply Blending Solution to an applicator or cotton ball, then dab onto canvas. Let dry.
2. Using a paintbrush, draw small circles on the canvas with Blending Solution. Let dry.

**Jen del Muro**

Jen is a life-long crafter with a passion for paper. She enjoys rubber stamping and dimension. She shares projects on her blog and teaches at ***Imprints*** in Ft Worth, TX.
www.iheart2stamp.com

**Donna Goss**

Donna has mastered many techniques to enhance her rubber stamp art and mixed media. She loves to read and teaches classes at ***Stamp Asylum*** in Plano, TX.
donnagoss@verizon.net

**Paula Phillips**

Paula is an innovative designer who loves all types of crafting. She has been designing for over 10 years, teaches classes and is also a digital designer.
paulaphillips.blogspot.com

**Barbara Buechley**

Barbara is an artist, professional painter and designer from DeSoto, TX. She does demos and teaches workshops, homeschool and art classes.
thecreativedoor.com

Birds on a Wire - page 18

*Great Looks with Sticky Canvas... Coloring Designs*

Bird on a Branch - page 17

## Colors on Sticky-Back Canvas

*by Donna Goss*

*I love Sticky-Back Canvas for several reasons. It comes with its own adhesive, it is easy to use and it sticks to almost anything.*

*Also, because of the paper backing, the canvas can be texturized. Simply layer it in an embossing folder and press using a Cuttlebug or Sizzix machine.*

**Suzanne McNeill**

Suzanne shares her creativity, designs,and enthusiasm in best-selling books by ***Design Originals***. Suzanne's mission is to publish quality books that inspire others to learn about fresh ideas and to experience the newest techniques, all the best projects and the most popular products.

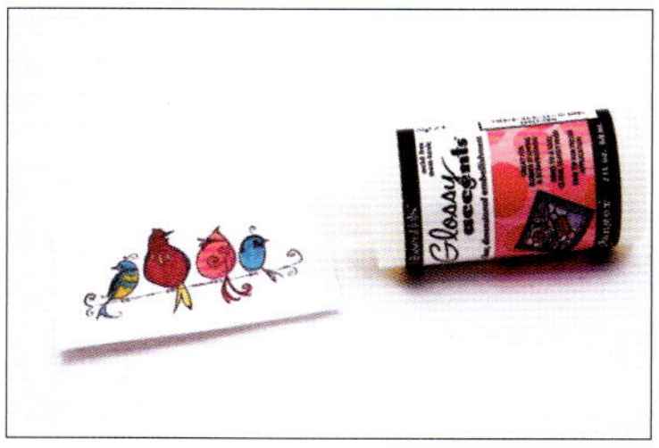

*Just like on cardstock, you can easily color and shade small designs with Permanent Markers. I like to use markers from Copic because they are available in a wide range of beautiful colors.*

**Coloring on Sticky-Back Canvas**

1. Stamp birds onto canvas using Black StazOn ink. Color birds with markers from *Copic,* being careful near the edge so the colors do not bleed outside the lines.Clean up any bleeds with Blending Solution on a swab stick or apply White paint over the area with a small brush.
2. Apply Glossy Accents from *Ranger* to the birds for sparkle. Let dry.